Linda J. Marlow
12/95

from Scott & Kimberley
at Christmas

HORSES

HORSES

An Illustrated Treasury

Compiled by Michelle Lovric

COURAGE BOOKS

an imprint of
RUNNING PRESS
Philadelphia, Pennsylvania

Royle

Copyright © 1994 by Royle Publications Limited
Royle House
Wenlock Road
London N1 7ST
England
Concept developed by Michelle Lovric
53 Shelton Street
Covent Garden
London WC2H 9HE
England

Canadian representatives: General Publishing Co., Ltd.,
30 Lesmill Road, Don Mills, Ontario M3B 2T6.

9 8 7 6 5 4 3 2 1
Digit on the right indicates the number of this printing.

Library of Congress Cataloging-in-Publication Number 93–72694

ISBN 1–56138–373–2

Cover design by Toby Schmidt
Cover illustration by Lucy Kemp-Welch
Interior design by Christian Benton
Edited by Melissa Stein
Typography by Deborah Lugar

Published by Courage Books, an imprint of
Running Press Book Publishers
125 South Twenty-second Street
Philadelphia, Pennsylvania 19103–4399

The author gratefully acknowledges the permission of the following
to reproduce copyrighted material in this book:
P. 18: From "The Foaling Time," translated by David Wevill from
The Boy Who Changed Into a Stag (Selected Poems 1949–1967) by
Ferenc Juhasz, published by Oxford University Press, Canada, in
1970, by permission of Artisjus, Le Bureau Hongrois pour la
Protection des Droits d'Auteur. Copyright © 1970 Ferenc Juhasz.
P. 20 and p. 22: From "Foal" and "Mare" by Vernon Phillips
Watkins, from *Unity of the Stream*, published by the English language
section of Yr Academi Gymreig in 1978. Copyright ©
Gwen Watkins.
P. 30: From *Venus Observed* by Christopher Fry, published in Great
Britain and the United States by Oxford University Press.
Copyright © 1950 Christopher Fry.
P. 44: From "Horses of the Camargue" by Roy Campbell,
reprinted courtesy of Francisco Campbell Custodio and AD.
Donker (Pty) Ltd.
P. 44: From "The Face of the Horse" from *Scrolls* by Nikolai
Alekseevich Zabolotsky, translated by Daniel Weissbort, published
by Jonathan Cape. Copyright © The Estate of Nikolai Alekseevich
Zabolotsky.
P. 47: From "The Horse" by Ronald Duncan, published by Souvenir
Press in 1981. Copyright © 1981 The Ronald Duncan Foundation.
Permission courtesy of Eric Glass Ltd.

Introduction .

Horses, swift and strong, have carried our history on their broad backs. Our most precious charges, our most urgent messages, our hopes and our fears have been entrusted to the horse. Nothing can quite compare to the horse's fluid lines, the sound of its thundering gallop, and the intuitive rapport between rider and mount.

Horses are the heroes and beloved friends of those whom they serve. The nature of the horse is filled with paradox: what other animal personifies pure power without aggression, possesses dignity with such gentle humility, and embodies both surging speed and endless patience? The same beast of burden that helps us farm the land once provided a noble alliance in battle and also offers a dream-escape for the leisure rider.

We have taken the image of the horse deep into our own language: our passions are "unbridled"; we can succeed if our spirits remain "unbroken"; we aspire to be "well-groomed." The ungainly first steps of the foal and its subsequent breaking-in have become metaphors for these stages in our own lives.

Horse's hooves have stirred our souls, and writers and artists celebrate the sleek, prancing poetry of the horse.

AND THE HOOFS OF
THE HORSES AS THEY RUN SHAKE THE
CRUMBLING FIELD. . . .

Virgil [Publius Virgilius Maro] (70–19 B.C.)
Roman poet

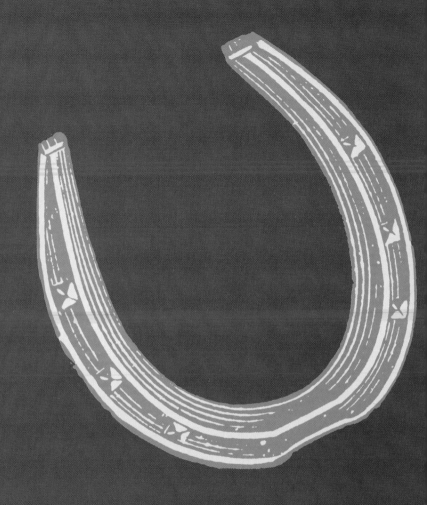

I am the Turquoise Woman's Son.
On top of Belted Mountain
beautiful horses—slim like a weasel!
My horse with a hoof like a striped agate,
with his fetlock like a fine eagle plume:
my horse whose legs are like quick lightning
whose body is an eagle-plumed arrow:
my horse whose tail is like a trailing black cloud.
The Little Holy Wind blows through his hair.
My horse with a mane made of short rainbows.
My horse with ears made of round corn.
My horse with eyes made of big stars.
My horse with a head made of mixed waters.
My horse with teeth made of white shell.
The long rainbow is in his mouth for a bridle
*   and with it I guide him.*

"THE WAR GOD'S HORSE SONG"
ANONYMOUS NAVAJO POET

. . . his hoofbeats fall like rain

Over and over and over again.

RACHEL FIELD (1894–1942)
AMERICAN POET

UNDER HIS SPURNING FEET, THE ROAD

LIKE AN ARROWLY ALPINE RIVER FLOWED;

AND THE LANDSCAPE SPED AWAY BEHIND

LIKE AN OCEAN FLYING BEFORE THE WIND. . . .

Thomas Buchanan Read (1822–1872)
American poet

What a piece of work is a horse! How noble in reasons! How infinite in faculty! In form and moving how express and admirable! In action how like an angel! In apprehension how like a man! The beauty of the world! The paragon of animals!

JAMES AGATE (1877–1947)
ENGLISH CRITIC AND ESSAYIST

*N*oblest of the train that wait on man, the flight-performing horse.

WILLIAM COWPER (1731–1800)
ENGLISH POET

WHEN I BESTRIDE HIM, I SOAR, I AM A

HAWK: HE TROTS THE AIR; THE EARTH

SINGS WHEN HE TOUCHES IT; THE

BASEST HORN OF HIS HOOF IS MORE

MUSICAL THAN THE PIPE OF HERMES.

William Shakespeare (1564–1616)
English playwright and poet

She was iron-sinew'd and
    satin-skinn'd,
Ribb'd like a drum and limb'd like
    a deer,
Fierce as the fire and fleet as the
    wind—
There was nothing she couldn't
    climb or clear.

ADAM LINDSAY GORDON (1833–1870)
AUSTRALIAN POET

My Beautiful! my beautiful! that standest meekly by

With thy proudly-arch'd and glossy neck, and dark and fiery eye,

Fret not to roam the desert now, with all thy winged speed;

I may not mount on thee again–thou'rt sold, my Arab steed!

CAROLINE NORTON (1808–1877)
IRISH WRITER

THE HORSE HAS SO DOCILE A NATURE,
THAT HE WOULD ALWAYS RATHER DO
RIGHT THAN WRONG, IF HE CAN ONLY
BE TAUGHT TO DISTINGUISH ONE FROM
THE OTHER.

George Melville (1821–1878)
Scottish writer

Dawn bounced up in a bright red hat,
waved at the world and skipped away.
Up staggered the foal,
its hooves were jelly-knots of foam.

Then day sniffed with its blue nose
through the open stable window, and found them—
the foal nuzzling its mother,
velvet fumbling for her milk.

FERENC JUHASZ, B. 1928
HUNGARIAN POET

A fine little

smooth horse colt,

Should move a man

as much as doth a son.

THOMAS KYD (1558–1594)
ENGLISH DRAMATIST

WHOEVER WATCHES A FOAL SEES TWO IMAGES,

DELICATE, CIRCLING, BORN, THE SPIRIT WITH BLIND EYES LEAPING

AND THE LEFT SPIRIT, VANISHED, YET HERE, THE VESSEL OF AGES

CLAY-COLD, BLUE LAID LOW BY HER GREAT WIDE BELLY THE HILL.

SEE HIM BREAK THAT CIRCLE, STOOPING TO DRINK, TO SUCK

HIS MOTHER, VAULTED WITH A BEAUTIFUL HERO'S BACK

ARCHED UNDER THE SINGING MANE. . . .

AND HE SLIPS FROM THAT MOTHER TO THE BOUNDLESS HORIZONS OF AIR,

LOOKING FOR THAT OTHER, THE FOAL NO LONGER THERE.

BUT PERHAPS

IN THE DARKNESS UNDER THE TUFTED THYME AND DOWNTRODDEN WINDS,

IN THE DARKNESS UNDER THE VIOLET'S ROOTS, IN THE DARKNESS OF THE PITCHER'S MUSIC,

IN THE UTTERMOST DARKNESS OF A VASE

THERE IS STILL THE PRINT OF FINGERS, THE SHADOW OF WATERS.

AND UNDER THE DRY, CURLED PARCHMENT OF THE SOIL THERE IS ALWAYS A LITTLE FOAL

ASLEEP.

Vernon Phillips Watkins (1906–1967)
Welsh poet

[The mare] set off for home with the speed of a swallow, and going as smoothly and silently. I never had dreamed of such delicate motion, fluent and graceful, and ambient, soft as the breeze flitting over the flowers, but swift as the summer lightning.

RICHARD DODDRIDGE BLACKMORE (1825–1900)
ENGLISH WRITER

The mare lies down in the grass where the nest of the skylark is hidden.

Her eyes drink the delicate horizon moving behind the song.

Deep sink the skies, a well of voices. Her sleep is the vessel of Summer.

VERNON WATKINS (1906–1967)
WELSH POET

$\mathcal{D}$O NOT SPUR A FREE HORSE.

Latin proverb

Then we began to ride. My soul

Smoothed itself out, a long-cramped scroll

Freshening and fluttering in the wind. . . .

ROBERT BROWNING (1812–1889)
ENGLISH POET

Oh, that ride! that first ride!—most truly it was an epoch in my existence; and I still look back to it with feelings of longing and regret. People·may talk of first love—it is a very agreeable event, I dare say—but give me the flush, and triumph, and glorious sweat of a first ride.

GEORGE BORROW (1803–1881)
ENGLISH WRITER AND LINGUIST

HE FLUNG HIMSELF ON HIS HORSES AND

RODE OFF MADLY IN ALL DIRECTIONS.

Stephen Butler Leacock (1869–1944)
English-born Canadian writer

If I be once on horse-back, I alight very unwillingly; for it is the seat I like best.

MICHEL EYQUEM DE MONTAIGNE (1533–1592)
FRENCH WRITER

H e that would venture nothing must not get on horseback.

SPANISH PROVERB

"BRING FORTH THE HORSE!"—THE HORSE WAS BROUGHT:

IN TRUTH, HE WAS A NOBLE STEED.

A TARTAR OF THE UKRAINE BREED,

WHO LOOK'D AS THOUGH THE SPEED OF THOUGHT

WERE IN HIS LIMBS. . . .

George Gordon, Lord Byron (1788–1824)
English poet

And still we galloped on from gorse to gorse,

And once, when checked, a thrush sang, and my horse

Pricked his quick ears as to a sound unknown.

I knew the Spring was come, I knew it even

Better than all by this, that through my chase

In bush and stone and hill and sea and heaven

It seemed to see and follow still your face.

Your face my quarry was, for it I rode,

My horse a thing of wings, myself a God.

WILFRED SCAWEN BLUNT (1840–1922)
ENGLISH POET

The air of heaven is that which blows between a horse's ears.

ARAB PROVERB

HORSES IT ALWAYS SEEMS

TO ME, ARE HALF A DREAM, EVEN WHEN

YOU HAVE THEM UNDER YOUR HAND AND WHEN I *DREAM* THEM

THEY TREMBLE AND SWEAT, THE CAVES OF THEIR NOSTRILS BLOWING

BRIGHT CLOUDS OF BREATH, A FOAMING SEA

BREAKS AGAINST THEIR MOUTHS, THEIR FLANKS ARE SMOKING

LIKE ABEL'S FIRE TO HEAVEN, AS THOUGH

A DREADFUL NECESSITY HAD RIDDEN THEM HARD

THROUGH THE MILES OF MY SLEEP, ALL THE BENIGHTED WAY

FROM LEGEND INTO LIFE. AND THEN IN THE MORNING

THERE THEY ARE IN THE STABLES, WAITING TO BE BLESSED.

Christopher Fry, b. 1907
English playwright

We attended the stables, as we

attended church, in our best

clothes, thereby no doubt showing

the degree of respect due to horses

and to the deity.

SIR OSBERT SITWELL (1892–1969)
ENGLISH WRITER

The wanton courser oft, with reins unbound,

Breaks from his stall, and beats the trembling ground;

Pamper'd and proud, he seeks the wonted tides,

And laves, in height of blood, his shining sides. . . .

HOMER (C. 1000 B.C.)
GREEK POET

$\mathcal{A}$ND ALLAH CREATED

OF THE HANDFUL OF WIND A HORSE

OF A CHESTNUT COLOR, LIKE GOLD,

AND SAID TO THE HORSE: BEHOLD I

HAVE CREATED THEE AND MADE THEE

ARABIAN, AND THOU SHALT HAVE

STATION AND POWER ABOVE ALL

THINGS OF THE BEASTS THAT ARE

SUBJECT TO MAN. AND I HAVE

BOUND ALL FORTUNE AND TREASURE

TO THY LOINS AND ON THY BACK A

RICH SPOIL, AND TO THY FORELOCK

A FAIR ISSUE. AND ALLAH SET LOOSE

THE SWIFT RUNNER AND HE WENT

ON HIS WAY NEIGHING.

Bedouin legend

Imperiously he leaps, he neighs, he bounds,
　　And now his woven girths he breaks asunder;
The bearing earth with his hard hoof he wounds;
　　Whose hollow womb resounds like heaven's thunder;
　　The iron bit he crusheth 'tween his teeth,
　　Controlling what he was controlled with.

WILLIAM SHAKESPEARE (1564–1616)
ENGLISH PLAYWRIGHT AND POET

The horse! The horse! The symbol of
surging potency and power of
movement, of action, in man.

D. H. LAWRENCE (1885–1930)
ENGLISH WRITER

A GIGANTIC BEAUTY OF A STALLION, FRESH AND RESPONSIVE TO MY CARESSES,

HEAD HIGH IN THE FOREHEAD, WIDE BETWEEN THE EARS,

LIMBS GLOSSY AND SUPPLE, TAIL DUSTING THE GROUND,

EYES FULL OF SPARKLING WICKEDNESS, EARS FINELY CUT, FLEXIBLY MOVING.

HIS NOSTRILS DILATE AS MY HEELS EMBRACE HIM,

HIS WELL-BUILT LIMBS TREMBLE WITH PLEASURE AS WE RACE AROUND

    AND RETURN. . . .

Walt Whitman (1819–1892)
American poet

The heart of the steed and the
heart of the master were beating
like prisoners assaulting
their walls. . . .

THOMAS BUCHANAN READ (1822–1872)
AMERICAN POET

To-night the very horses springing by

Toss gold from whitened nostrils. In a dream

The streets that narrow to the westward gleam

Like rows of golden palaces; and high

From all the crowded chimneys tower and die

A thousand aureoles. . . .

ARCHIBALD LAMPMAN (1861–1899)
CANADIAN POET

MEN ARE BETTER WHEN RIDING, MORE JUST AND MORE
UNDERSTANDING, AND MORE ALERT AND MORE AT EASE
AND MORE UNDER-TAKING, AND BETTER KNOWING OF
ALL COUNTRIES AND ALL PASSAGES; IN SHORT AND
LONG ALL GOOD CUSTOMS AND MANNERS COMETH
THEREOF, AND THE HEALTH OF MAN AND OF HIS SOUL.

Edward Plantagenet, Second Duke of York (1373–1415)

The trot is the foundation of the gallop.

RICHARD BERENGER (1720–1782)
ENGLISH WRITER AND GENTLEMAN OF THE HORSE TO GEORGE III

forty

A canter is the cure for every evil.

BENJAMIN DISRAELI (1804–1881)
ENGLISH STATESMAN

HAST THOU GIVEN THE HORSE STRENGTH? HAS THOU CLOTHED HIS NECK

WITH THUNDER?

CANST THOU MAKE HIM AFRAID AS A GRASSHOPPER?

THE GLORY OF HIS NOSTRILS IS TERRIBLE.

HE PAWETH IN THE VALLEY, AND REJOICETH IN *HIS* STRENGTH: HE GOES ON TO

MEET THE ARMED MEN.

HE MOCKETH AT FEAR, AND IS NOT AFFRIGHTED; NEITHER TURNETH HE BACK

FROM THE SWORD.

The Bible, *Job 39:19–22*

*They say
that princes learn no art truly,
but the art of horsemanship.
The reason is, the brave beast is
no flatterer. He will throw a prince
as soon as his groom.*

Ben Jonson (1572–1637)
English dramatist

Horses carry the history of mankind on their backs. If you should find one is carrying you as well, acknowledge your good fortune and indeed your honour.

LUCINDA PRIOR PALMER, B. 1953
ENGLISH EQUESTRIAN

I HEARD A SUDDEN HARMONY OF HOOVES,

AND, TURNING, SAW AFAR

A HUNDRED SNOWY HORSES UNCONFINED,

THE SILVER RUNAWAYS OF NEPTUNE'S CAR

RACING, SPRAY-CURLED, LIKE WAVES BEFORE THE WIND.

Roy Campbell (1901–1957)
South African poet

And if a man should see

The horse's magical face,

He would tear out his own impotent tongue

And give it to the horse. For

This magical creature is surely worthy of it.

Then we should hear words.

Words large as apples. Thick

As honey or buttermilk.

Words which penetrate like flame. . . .

Words which do not die

And which we celebrate in song.

Nikolai Alekseevich Zabolotsky (1903–1958)
RUSSIAN WRITER

Far back, far back in our dark soul the horse prances.

D. H. LAWRENCE (1885–1930)
ENGLISH WRITER

. . . SHUT OUR EYES TIGHT AGAINST THIS HORSE,

BREATHE HIM IN,

CLOSE ON OUR NECKS HOT BREATH OF THE HORSE,

WHINNYING, STOMPING, GLISTENING HORSE . . .

NOW BEATING THE ROAD, BREAKING SHADOWS WITH ITS HOOVES,

SHADOW HORSE BLUE AS TREES, HUGE AS HOUSES. . . .

Justine Sydney
20th-century American poet

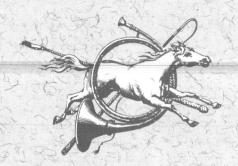

There is no secret so close as that
between a rider and his horse.

ROBERT SMITH SURTEES (1803–1864)
ENGLISH WRITER

This Cavalcade of Grace now stands,
    it speaks in silence.
Where in this wide world can
man find nobility without pride,
friendship without envy or beauty
without vanity? here, where
grace is laced with muscle, and
strength by gentleness confined. . . .

All our history is his
industry; we are his heirs, he
our inheritance.
Ladies and Gentlemen: The Horse!

Ronald Duncan, b. 1914
English poet and dramatist

ILLUSTRATION ACKNOWLEDGMENTS

TITLE PAGE [detail]: *Awaiting Instructions*, Rosemary Welch
(N E Middleton Limited)

p. 6: *Thundering Hooves*, Frank Wootton

p. 9: *A Bay Horse and a White Dog Near a Lake*,
George Stubbs

p. 10: *Arab Mares and Foals*, Lucy Kemp Welch
(David Messum Gallery)

p. 13: *Going to the Start—Newmarket*, Frank Wootton

p. 14: *Mancha*, Diana R. Lodge

p. 17: *The Classic Arab—Blenheim*, Frank Wootton

p. 19: *Young Foal Resting*, Frank Wootton

p. 21: *Grey Mare and Foal*, T. S. La Fontaine

p. 23: *In Dublin Bay*, Heywood Hardy
(Fine Art Photographic Library Limited)

p. 24: *The Inn Yard*, Sir Alfred Munnings
(Sir Alfred Munnings Art Museum, Dedham, Essex)

p. 27: *Schooling the Pony*, Sir John Lavery
(Rochdale Art Gallery)

p. 28: *Two Horses' Heads*, Frank Wootton

p. 31: *Paying the Ostler*, George Morland (Laing Art Gallery,
Newcastle upon Tyne, England (Tyne and Wear Museums))

p. 32: *Off to the Derby*, George Derville Rowlandson
(Fine Art Photographic Library Limited)

pp. 36–37: *Exercising Horses at Newbury—Summer*,
Frank Wootton

p. 39: *Morning on the Manton Downs*, Sir Alfred Munnings
(Sir Alfred Munnings Art Museum, Dedham, Essex)

p. 40: *Across the Beach*, Rosemary Welch
(N E Middleton Limited)

p. 43: *Mares and Foal by a Lake*, Frank Wootton

p. 45 [detail]: *Grey Stallion with Mares and Foals*,
George Stubbs

p. 47: *Bay Horse in Stable*, Robert Rasell